Praise ~~for~~
Bible Proofreading Service

One of our goals for Zondervan Bibles is creating the most excellent and trusted Bibles possible. Peachtree is a valued partner in that work. Because of their high attention to detail and dedication to excellence, we value their assistance in creating Bibles we can be proud to present to our readers.

—**Melinda Bouma**
VP & Publisher,
Zondervan Bibles

For well over a quarter of a century Peachtree has been a valued and reliable partner in helping us to produce the most accurate Bible texts possible. The forensic approach to proofreading coupled with the helpful editorial advice have made Peachtree a fundamental part of our process for developing new material.

—**Bob Groser**
Cambridge Bibles

I have been working with Peachtree Publishing Services for twenty-five years. Somehow they have always been able to work within my schedule to deliver extremely accurate proofread Bible settings in a number of different translations. They are simply the best at what they do!

—**Lloyd Mullins**
Managing Editor
LifeWay | Holman Bible and Reference

At 2K/Denmark we work on close to 100 Bibles annually, and our ambition is that each Bible is the best we have made. Peachtree matches our ambition for quality and is backed by an outstanding experience in the industry. They are clearly the best Bible proofreaders we have worked with.

—**Sune Anderson**
COO
2K/DENMARK

Peachtree is the Babe Ruth of Bible proofreading. During my years as the Associate Publisher and Acquisitions Editor, Bibles at HarperCollins Christian Publishing, we relied upon their stellar proofreading services. Highly recommended.

—**Bob DeMoss**
New York Times Bestselling Author

We know how important it is to get Bibles right, and that's why we trust Peachtree's experience and passion for our Bible proofreading.

—**Paul Muckley**
Barbour Bibles

Peachtree is our go-to partner for all of our Bible proofreading. Their Bible proofreading service is beyond comparison for checking editorial accuracy and enforcing consistency of style. We wouldn't think about going to print without first having them proof the individual books of the Bible.

—**Carlton Garborg**
President
Broadstreet Publishing

For many years, we've entrusted the proofreading of our Bibles to Peachtree Publishing Services. Peachtree's proofreaders do consistently excellent work: They perform thorough checks on a long list of detailed tasks for each book of the Bible, meet their deadlines and graciously adapt to schedule changes, respond well to feedback and ask good questions both up front and throughout the process, and make my team feel safe knowing they will catch errors that have so far gone unnoticed. We've worked with Peachtree on our biggest and most important Bibles in a variety of translations and have found the proofreaders to be careful, communicative, flexible, and a delight to work with—it's an honor and a joy to partner with them in the ministry of the gospel.

—**Sarah Johnson**
Copyediting Team Leader | Bibles & Alliances
Tyndale House Publishers

Peachtree Publishing Services is a valued publishing partner. Peachtree is dependable, trustworthy, and provides excellent editorial and proofing services for all of our publishing needs.

—**Joshua D. Green**
Associate Publisher
LifeWay | Holman Bible and Reference

During my forty-plus years working in the Bible publishing industry, I learned from and relied heavily on the expertise of the people at Peachtree Publishing Services. Not only were they professional partners who made my job easier and made the products we published succeed, but they were my friends!

—**Doris Rikkers**
Former Vice President/Publisher
Zondervan Bibles and World Publishing

Peachtree goes above and beyond our expectations time and time again, with focus, execution, first-rate quality, and timely completion. They are not a service, but true partners in ministry!

—**Matthew Elliott, PhD**
President, Oasis International
Publisher, Africa Study Bible

Peachtree has been proofreading Bible pages typeset by Livingstone for over 25 years. Their dedication to excellence gives us complete confidence when working with God's Word.

—**Ashley Taylor**
The Livingstone Corporation

We have worked with Peachtree Publishing Services on a variety of projects, and each time the results have been outstanding. Their experience, expertise, and attention to detail are extremely valuable at every point of the publishing process. They take the time to explore and understand our project expectations so that they can deliver exactly what we need with the best possible results. We look forward to many more projects with them in the future.

—**Pike Lambeth**
Executive Vice President
The Lockman Foundation

Team 316 is extremely grateful for the diligent work of Team Peachtree! Your thoroughness and timely communication allowed the first edition of the *Legacy Standard Bible* to cross the finish line on time!

The overused adage seems fitting: "We couldn't have done it without you!" We look forward to continuing our business relationship for many more projects together!

—**Chris Scotti**
VP and Publisher
Three Sixteen Publishing

We have been publishing books for many decades, and yet when we decided to publish Bibles, it felt like we had to relearn everything afresh. Eventually we decided to work with some real experts and hired Peachtree to manage everything. It was a great decision, one that has paid off in many ways.

—**Michael G. Maudlin**
SVP and Executive Editor
HarperOne

I have been involved with Peachtree Publishing Services for many years. For every project they deliver a tremendous sense of professionalism, value, and, most importantly, accuracy and timeliness. This team is simply the best at what they do.

—**Wayne Hastings**
Consultant, Bible Editor, and Publisher
The Wayne Hastings Company

Peachtree Publishing Services continues to serve our publishing work with the highest level of skill. PPS has proven to be trustworthy at every turn and I'm proud to have them serve our publishing work.

—**Philip Nation,**
Vice-President/Publisher
Thomas Nelson Bibles

Peachtree's Bible proofreading services are excellent. Their team is professional, courteous, and responsive and meets their schedule.

—**Jeana Ledbetter**
Associate Publisher
Hachette Book Group

As a publisher, getting it right for an author is stressful enough. But then, what about when the author is God? That's where I lean on Peachtree to ensure we get it right, accurate, and without error. Because of Peachtree as a partner in Bible publishing, I don't lie awake at nights.

What I love about Peachtree is that when they pick up a project with us, it's like they are vested owners and treat it as importantly as we do. We don't feel like a customer; we feel like a partner.

Peachtree has been my go-to partner for anything Bible-publishing related for over two decades. Not only are they experts in the Bible space delivering excellence on time, they are also passionate about God's Word, which is something you just can't buy.

—Jason Rovenstine
VP of New Business Development
DaySpring

Peachtree has proofread several of our Bible projects with great speed and careful attention to detail. We are very grateful for their partnership!

—Alyssa Roten
Technical Art Designer
Life Publishers

Tyndale has relied on Peachtree's English Bible proofreading service for decades, and we have recently begun using their Spanish Bible proofreading service as well. Peachtree has been proactive in learning the nuances of the translations we publish, and we are entirely pleased with their attention to detail and collaborative spirit.
—Spanish Editorial Services
Tyndale House Publishers

When I was a new Bibles editor, the team was instrumental in helping me learn the Bible production process. And their notes and comments on my proofs were an education in and of themselves. As a more seasoned editor, I find that I still keep learning from the team. The direct effect of working with the Peachtree editing and proofreading teams is that they helped me produce some projects I'm quite proud of. The indirect result is that they have made me a better all-around editor.

—Jill M. Smith
Writer, Ghostwriter, Editor
Former Senior Editor, Thomas Nelson Bibles

Being a part of proofing a Bible for the first time has been absolutely eye-opening to me and the rest of the team. The work you all do is absolutely astounding and valuable beyond words.

—Nick Guiliano
Hosanna Revival

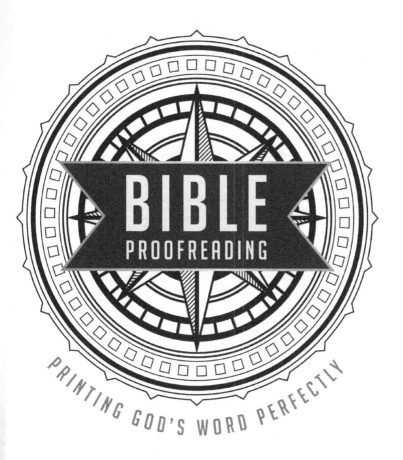

BIBLE
PROOFREADING

PRINTING GOD'S WORD PERFECTLY

Peachtree
PUBLISHING SERVICES

Contents

In honor of
Mildred, Doug, and June:

Your drive for perfection
still inspires us.

The Eternal Impact of Bible Proofreading

"Thank you for proofreading my Bible."

Imagine our surprise to get an unexpected, unsolicited word of gratitude from a man named Arlyn. He found out that, among our varied services, Peachtree proofreads Bibles for many of the world's top Bible publishers. Arlyn then proceeded to do something very few people do. He reached out with a message of heartfelt gratitude. This is what he said:

> I've had my Bible for twenty years, and I read it every day. Until recently it never occurred to me that someone read these pages before me—to make sure that my Bible was free from errors. Over the years I've found many truths in these pages. I've found God's care for me. I've

found conviction. I found faith. But the one thing I never found was a typo.

Want to guess how much that simple, short message encouraged our team?

Our Bible proofreaders work daily to ensure every Bible we work on is free of error. Compared to a global disaster, a typo seems inconsequential, doesn't it? But that's not the case.

"Over the years I've found many truths in these pages. I've found God's care for me. I've found conviction. I found faith. But the one thing I never found was a typo."

Remember how frequently Jesus emphasized the importance of small things—toddlers, a poor woman's meager offering, faith the size of the minuscule mustard seed? His point seemed to be that more often than not, it's the littlest, most overlooked things that God uses in the most powerful ways.

Take, for example, the Christian restaurant worker at the franchise up the road. She's only making minimum wage—why is she so joyful? Because she knows she's not merely making sandwiches. She's making it possible for a dad to meet his college-aged daughter for a quick lunch and an important conversation. She's helping a frazzled, single mom feed her two kids on a busy school night.

In the same way, Peachtree's Bible proofreaders know that they're doing much more than circling mistakes with red pens. They're finding and eliminating avoidable distractions so that Bible readers can engage God Almighty. And that's a big, important mission.

The thoughtful message we received from Arlyn confirmed that our work matters. Catching errors makes an eternal difference. Because we carefully proofed his Bible, he has been able to meet with God every day for twenty years. Never once did he find a mistake that hijacked his thoughts or undermined his ability to trust what was printed on the page.

[We're] finding and eliminating avoidable distractions so that Bible readers can engage God Almighty. And that's a big, important mission.

And consider this: In the United States alone, more than twenty million Bibles are sold and distributed each year. Each one of those copies of God's Word ends up somewhere—in a bedroom or dorm room, a hotel room or prison cell. God only knows how many lives, how many Arlyns, will be touched by all those copies and versions of the Holy Scriptures.

The Bible should be printed without typos that distract readers from God's message.

1

Is There a Typo in Your Bible?

"There's a Bible verse missing."

There are few sentences that strike more fear in a Bible publisher's heart than the one above. First, there's the theological reason: Doesn't God's Word *deserve* to be printed perfectly? Second, there's the personal reason: How did this mistake get past me? And third, there's the business reason: What will we do with thousands of printed Bibles that contain a glaring and distracting typo?

Real reasons like this motivate our Bible proofreading team to find mistakes, dropped words, and missing verses in every Bible we work on. While the world's best and biggest Bible publishers produce dozens of Bibles a year, we often see that even the most experienced staff make small mistakes that can prove costly if they are not caught.

Today's databases and typesetters are very good but there is still room for errors. As a business dedicated to proofreading Bibles, we can tell you that we find errors in page layouts every day in Bibles before they go to print.

this | And let him that heareth say, Come. And let him that is athirst come. And whosoever
ard | will, let him take the water of life freely.
fell | 18 For I testify unto every man that heareth
ngel | the words of the prophecy of this book, If any man shall add unto these things, God
not: | shall add unto him the plagues that are
eth- | written in this book:
eep | (19) And if any man shall take away from the words of the book of this prophecy, God
say- | shall take away his part out of the book of
the | life, and out of the holy city, and *from* the things which are written in this book. → *missing verse 20*
till: | (21) The grace of our Lord Jesus Christ *be* with you all. Amen.
till: |
igh- |
be |

Bible proofreading should ensure that every verse is present.

Doesn't God's Word deserve to be printed perfectly?

The Importance of Bible Proofreading

Wise King Solomon famously wrote, "When there are many words, transgression is unavoidable" (Proverbs 10:19 NASB95). He was referring to the spoken word—suggesting the more we run our mouths, the more likely we are to say something wrong.

But here's what every publisher and editor and proofreader knows: Solomon's keen observation applies equally to written words.

Consider: If it's possible for one short word to contain a typo, how many mistakes can creep in when you tackle the 1,189 chapters, 31,012 verses, and 785,000+ words of a new Bible project?

We find errors in page layouts every day in Bibles before they go to print.

Add to that new project thousands of study notes and dozens of other explanatory features, and every new study or devotional Bible becomes the perfect storm for slip-ups. Five misspellings here, seven typos there. Omitted words. Extra words. Wrong punctuation marks—or none at all. The potential errors are limitless.

It's a big deal. Why? Because each mistake has the potential to distract readers from God's message. Instead of encountering God, they're fixated on an error. Truly, getting a Bible project right is a high and holy spiritual duty. Here are the three reasons every Bible publisher desperately needs an investment in quality Bible proofreading.

1. Mistakes are inevitable.

People—even those perfectionists among us—are less than perfect. That's not a judgment; it's a fact. The mind can focus intensely only for so long before it begins to wander. And when the eyes begin to tire, they can't possibly notice every inaccuracy. This is when oversights occur. And it's when a few seconds of *careless* can ruin months and months of *careful*.

Each mistake has the potential to distract readers from God's message.

What's more, because humans are mistake-prone, the systems and software we devise to catch errors aren't always foolproof either. Alas, our creations bear our image. To be sure, spell-check and grammar programs get better all the time. Nevertheless we inhabit a world where glitches—mental, mechanical, and digital—are commonplace.

History's most infamous example? Here's

a vote for a Bible publishing project in 1631. Robert Barker and Martin Lucas decided to print and sell a thousand copies of the Good Book. But because of a typesetting blunder (some suspect sabotage at the hands of a rival printer), Barker and Lucas ended up producing the notorious Wicked Bible instead. Imagine how horrified these men were when they realized their fancy new Bible commanded, "Thou shalt commit adultery" (Exodus 20:14)!

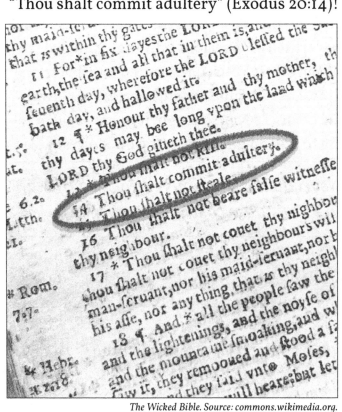

The Wicked Bible. Source: commons.wikimedia.org.

2. Mistakes are costly.

The omission of the word "not" in the seventh of the Ten Commandments cost Barker and Lucas dearly. All but a handful of their hot-off-the-press "Wicked" Bibles were burned. The men were hauled into court, fined by King Charles I, and forced to surrender their printing licenses. Poor Barker (*literally* poor) eventually died in a debtors' prison.

Today we don't have to fear a stint in a debtors' prison for committing such a mistake. Nevertheless a serious editorial gaffe can result in costly consequences: Lost respect. Lost time. Lost revenue. Potentially lost jobs. And if the error is severe enough, it might mean having to pull an entire printing off store shelves.

Nevertheless a serious editorial gaffe can result in costly consequences.

And worst of all? Readers who open their Bibles to hear from God are distracted. They miss a divine message because of human error.

Bibles are too important to print with careless errors.

3. Mistakes are catchable.

Okay, so mistakes are bound to happen. And some of those errors can prove to be costly. But here's the third reality—an encouraging

---

Bibles are too important to print with careless errors.

---

fact: Mistakes are catchable. What's more, they're correctable in the early stages of Bible production, before they do a lot of damage.

Every Bible publishing project has at least 300,000 details that need to be checked.

2

How to Avoid a Costly Bible Publishing Disaster

Painful errors can usually be avoided.

Do apples, cinnamon, and Parmesan go together? Well, that's a matter of personal taste. But chances are, you don't expect to see that mix of flavors in your Bible.

It's a fact of life and business. Equipment breaks down. Software gets glitchy. Employees get distracted or weary or sloppy. If a business doesn't have trustworthy quality control systems in place, it could be headed for a worst-case scenario—a costly problem.

Unfortunately, Bible publishing isn't exempt from these grim realities. Over the years we've heard all sorts of horror stories of expensive mistakes not caught before a new Bible project went to press. Check out these actual Bible publishing nightmares. (Note: We've withheld publishers' names and allowed years to go by to avoid causing embarrassment.)

Lorem Ipsum 15:1

We know one Bible that featured the Latin text printed on the last page of Hosea. An inadvertent shortcut key pasted the text just before the Bible went to the printer. Ten thousand Bibles were recalled. You don't need a calculator to figure out the bottom line there: no ministry and an immense expense.

Hosea 14

2 Take with you words, and turn to the Lord: say unto him, Take away all iniquity, and receive us graciously: so will we render the calves of our lips.
3 Asshur shall not save us; we will not ride upon horses: neither will we say any more to the work of our hands, Ye are our gods: for in thee the fatherless findeth mercy.
4 I will heal their backsliding, I will love them freely: for mine anger is turned away from him.
5 I will be as the dew unto Israel: he shall grow as the lily, and cast forth his roots as Lebanon.
6 His branches shall spread, and his beauty shall be as the olive tree, and his smell as Leb-

things? prudent, and he shall know them? for the ways of the Lord are right, and the just shall walk in them: but the transgressors shall fall therein.
Lorem ipsum dolor sit amet, consectetur adipiscing elit, sed do eiusmod tempor incididunt ut labore et dolore magna aliqua. Pharetra convallis posuere morbi leo urna molestie at elementum eu. Amet volutpat consequat mauris nunc congue nisi. Sagittis vitae et leo duis ut diam. Vivamus at augue eget arcu dictum. Vel eros donec ac odio tempor orci. Morbi tristique senectus et netus et malesuada. Volutpat est velit egestas dui id ornare. Nunc non blandit massa enim nec dui nunc mattis

Accidental text inserted into a printed Bible can be a costly error.

Let Go a Month Too Late

Then there was the disgruntled employee who was being fired by his publishing company. As his parting act, the man intentionally deleted a verse from the book of Revelation. No one noticed before the Bible was printed.

We Knew We Forgot Something!

How about the small publishing house that was banking its entire future on a big, ambitious new Bible project—a brand-new translation. The translation carried a big price tag and a monumental flaw. The beautiful page design did not include running heads. Without these summary headers at the top of each page, the Bible was impossible to use, especially for new believers and pre-believers. This costly project never got word-of-mouth traction. As a result, it's a translation you've never heard of.

"You proofread Bibles, right?"

Those were the words one of our team members heard as someone ran up to him after church. The person caught up to him and said, "Look what I found in my Bible!" He opened to the Gospel of Luke and displayed a page with an inconsistent use of fonts. While we hadn't been asked to proofread that Bible, we were still sad for the reader. He had opened God's Word that morning hoping to find spiritual insights. Instead, he found a distracting mess and completely missed the message.

He had opened God's Word that morning hoping to find spiritual insights. Instead, he found a distracting mess and completely missed the message.

A Cat on the Keyboard?

While we never asked for an explanation, here is a snapshot of a Bible that came to us for proofreading. While working from home has its perks for typesetters, sometimes it also comes with working with pets. What else would cause random keystrokes like this?

JOSHUA COMMISSIONED

1 Now after the death of Moses the servant of the Lord it came to pass, that the Lord spake unto Joshua the son of Nun, Moses' min____, saying,

2 Moses my servant is dea#ASDd; now therefore arise, go ver this Jordan, thou, and all this people, unto the land which I do giv to them, evOKJHen to the children o Israel.

3 Every place that the ole of your fot shll tre@#$%^ad pon, that have I given unto you, as I said unto Moses.

4 From the wilderness and this Lebanon even unto the great river, the river Euphrates, all the land of the Hittites, and unto the great sea toward the going down of the sun, shall be your coast.

5 There shall not any man be able to stand before thee all the days of thy life: as I was with Moses, so I will be with thee: I will not fail thee, nor forsake thee.

6 Be strong and of a good courage: for unto this people shalt thou divide for an inheritance the land, which I sware unto their fathers to give them.

Paragraph Markers

And then there was the influx of customer complaints that a new Bible publisher experienced. The publisher was criticized for manipulating the beloved King James Bible. The specific complaint? Words were not correctly italicized and some of the paragraph indicators were missing. By the time the publisher called us for a thorough proofread, tens of thousands of Bibles had already rolled off the presses, generating emails, calls, and complaints.

"Want a little Parmesan with that psalm?"

Where is your go-to place for saving a favorite recipe? What about the cross-reference column of your Bible? That's what one typesetter did, albeit accidentally. It seems the typesetter unknowingly pasted portions of a recipe that had been copied during a lunch break right into the cross-reference section of a project. Our team found the mistake in our normal proofing process and a crisis was averted.

```
thinketh upon me: thou art my help and my
deliverer; make no tarrying, O my God.                    4
                                                         out
   To the chief Musician, A Psalm of David.   2 Isa.     mu
41  Blessed is he that considereth the       49:24;      Go
    poor: the LORD will deliver him in time   Combine     mu
of trouble.                                   bread
                                              crumbs,     5
2  The LORD will preserve him, and kee        Italian     wh
him alive; and he shall be blessed upon th    seasoning
earth: and thou wilt not deliver him unto th  and garlic  Go
will of his enemies.                          powder in   his
                                              shallow
3  The LORD will strengthen him upon th       dish. Dip   6
bed of languishing: thou wilt make all his be chicken in  me
in his sickness.                              egg, then   lan
4  I said, LORD, be merciful unto me: hea     crumb       the
my soul; for I have sinned against thee.      mixture;    7
5  Mine enemies speak evil of me, When        turn to     wa
shall he die, and his name perish?            coat. 2.    are
6  And if he come to see me, he speaketh      Arrange      8
vanity: his heart gathereth iniquity to itself; chicken   gk
                                              in 13 x      nic
                                              9-inch
                                              baking
```

Some Bibles have over 70,000 cross-references. This one also included a recipe for delicious Parmesan chicken. Our Scripture Integrity Team caught it at first pages.

While the above examples may be considered sensational, they are not atypical. They are, in fact, variants on a theme. Even the best and most careful typesetters and publishing partners are staffed by human beings. And each of us, no matter how careful, is susceptible to introducing an unexpected error that makes Bible proofreading absolutely necessary.

And each of us, no matter how careful, is susceptible to introducing an unexpected error that makes Bible proofreading absolutely necessary.

When it pertains to the Word of God and new Bible projects, quality control systems are especially important. To avoid embarrassing and costly mistakes, have your Bible proofread. Proofreading can help make sure all those t's are crossed and the i's are dotted—and not sprinkled with cinnamon.

Cutting costs by skipping proofing can turn out to be expensive.

3

Getting the Bible Right

Avoid that pesky one-star review.

If readers expect that just about every book will contain a typo or two, why are they so quick to post a one-star review if they find a mistake in their Bible?

The higher standard for Bible publishing stems from the readers' view of this sacred book. From the beginning of the Bible's history, the people of God have treated the written Word of God with the utmost care. Even Moses carefully guarded the newly received law of God by placing the original Ten Commandments into the ark of the covenant for safekeeping (see Deuteronomy 10:1–5).

That same determination to protect and preserve God's Word influenced generations of Hebrew scribes for thousands of years, as evidenced by the Masoretes, who treated their sacred scrolls "with the greatest imaginable reverence, and devised a complicated system of safeguards against scribal slips."[1] It is said that ancient scribes counted the number of times each letter of the alphabet was found in each book. They even went so far as to locate the letters that were in the exact middle of the Pentateuch and the Hebrew Bible, respectively.

Can you say *meticulous*?

That's not all. Hebrew legend indicates that if a scribe was copying the Torah by hand and discovered he had made a mistake, he stopped his work, put down his pen, and burned the scroll. The slightest human slip could—and did—lead to a monumental amount of rework.

This effort did not deter them because this was the reverence the ancients had for God's Word.

DIFFERENCES IN EXODUS

Each translation contains differences that must be proofread accordingly. Consider some of the subtle differences found between three popular translations of Exodus.

	NIV 2011	NASB 2020	NTV (SPANISH)
Number of times the word LORD or SEÑOR appears in small caps	409	399	426
Typical number of footnotes	129	79	172
Lines of poetry	76	49	77
Subheads	88	89	88

Today's Bible readers hold similar values. They believe that the book in their hands does not just contain words but is *the* Word. It is *God's* message that still speaks to their hearts and drives the way they live. As a result, perfection still matters when printing the Bible. Careful proofreading offers vital protection.

Below are four ways Bible proofreading serves readers and publishers.

1. Proofreading protects God's Word.

The Bible deserves to be protected because we believe it is God's revelation to the world. In the sacred texts of the Old and New Testaments, God shows us what he is like, what we are like, and what it means to have a relationship with him.

Our Scripture Integrity Team feels a powerful sense of responsibility whenever they sit down with the pages of a new Bible translation or project. We love God's Word and want others to be able to read divine truth without getting sidetracked by glaring human errors. We believe God's Word should be printed with excellent care so that people can engage it fully, accurately, and without distraction.

2. Proofreading protects readers.

Since the mission of most Bible publishers is to help people read God's Word, our proofing system is designed around that goal—to ensure that readers can discover God's message free of avoidable distractions. By proofreading Bibles, we help protect the investment of the people who purchase those Bibles while also guarding their hearts as they seek to know God better.

The Bible deserves to be protected because we believe it is God's revelation to the world.

3. Proofreading protects the copyright holder.

Because only a handful of translations are considered public domain, most translations are copyrighted to a publisher. In proofing Bibles, we are protecting the copyright holder of each Bible version. The translators carefully and intentionally chose certain words. They agonized over the formatting to use for every line of Scripture. And even if we love a new design provided by the publisher, we flag a page that deviates from copyright requirements. We have an obligation to protect the text—and the client.

The translators' thoughtful and deliberate wrestling with every matter leads to our strong sense of duty to honor their efforts. Our goal is to ensure that every Bible we work on preserves the translators' intent and protects the copyright and mission of the publishing partner.

Ezra

Cyrus Allows the Exiles to Return

1 In the first year of King Cyrus of Persia,* the LORD fulfilled the prophecy he had given through Jeremiah.* He stirred the heart of Cyrus to put this proclamation in writing and to send it throughout his kingdom:

² "This is what King Cyrus of Persia says:
"The LORD, the God of heaven, has given me all the kingdoms of the earth. He has appointed me to build him a Temple at Jerusalem, which is in Judah. ³ Any of you who are his people may go to Jerusalem in Judah to rebuild this Temple of the LORD, the God of Israel, who lives in Jerusalem. And may your God be with you! ⁴ Wherever this Jewish remnant is found, let their neighbors contribute toward their expenses by giving them silver and gold, supplies for the journey, and livestock, as well as a voluntary offering for the Temple of God in Jerusalem."

⁵ Then God stirred the hearts of the priests and Levites and the leaders of the tribes of Judah and Benjamin to go to Jerusalem to rebuild the Temple of the LORD. ⁶ And all their neighbors assisted by giving them articles of silver and gold, supplies for the journey, and livestock. They gave them many valuable gifts

¹¹ In all, there were 5,400 articles of gold and silver. Sheshbazzar brought all of these along when the exiles went from Babylon to Jerusalem.

Exiles Who Returned with Zerubbabel

2 Here is the list of the Jewish exiles of the provinces who returned from their captivity. King Nebuchadnezzar had deported them to Babylon, but now they returned to Jerusalem and the other towns in Judah where they originally lived. ²Their leaders were Zerubbabel, Jeshua, Nehemiah, Seraiah, Reelaiah, Mordecai, Bilshan, Mispar, Bigvai, Rehum, and Baanah.

This is the number of the men of Israel who returned from exile:
³ The family of Parosh. 2,172
⁴ The family of Shephatiah. 372
⁵ The family of Arah 775
⁶ The family of Pahath-moab
(descendants of Jeshua and Joab). . 2,812
⁷ The family of Elam. 1,254
⁸ The family of Zattu. 945
⁹ The family of Zaccai 760
¹⁰ The family of Bani 642
¹¹ The family of Bebai. 623
¹² The family of Azgad 1,222
¹³ The family of Adonikam 666
¹⁴ The family of Bigvai 2,056

Every list and alignment decision is made by the translators and must be maintained in every printing. The above example is from Ezra 1–2 (NLT).

4. Proofreading protects editors.

Printing a Bible that contains mistakes can lead to sleepless nights for a publishing team. Minor errors can lead to critical customers and bad reviews, while significant errors can lead to abandoned inventory and financial losses for the publisher.

Investing in quality proofreading requires hundreds of hours, but it can ensure that publishers avoid nightmares like these.

Being meticulous with the
Word of God matters.

[1] F. F. Bruce, *The Books and the Parchments*, Old Tappan, New Jersey: Fleming H. Revell Company, 1984, 108.

4

Why Do Bibles Still Need to Be Proofread?

Short answer: because you can't publish a Bible without human involvement.

Remember the Telephone game? You would whisper something to a friend, who would whisper it to another, who would whisper it to another, and so on. By the time it reached the end of the line, "I'll have french fries and a strawberry shake" had morphed into "All French spies hate berries and snakes."

Always good for a few laughs, the game also serves as a cautionary tale of what happens when people try to exchange information. The more times words are passed along, the more chances words can be changed.

Unfortunately, this is true even for Bible projects that are based in a digital workflow. You might think that as many times as popular Bible translations have been typeset, printed, and reprinted, publishers would have made—and caught—every mistake imaginable. Is there really a need for your Bible to be proofread?

Perhaps not if we had stuck with only one Bible translation, one typesetting, and one design. If Bible publishers had done that, we should now have a mistake-free, unchanging set of proofs to use for cranking out "perfect" Bibles.

But we don't have only one translation that's been typeset perfectly for perpetuity. There are hundreds of translations in English alone and dozens in Spanish, and portions of the Bible have been translated into thousands of other languages over the years.

The sorts of mistakes proofreaders watch for are varied and run the gamut from missing text to wrong wording to general typos.

Keeping Track of Updates

To complicate matters, publishers and translation teams are forever updating their Bibles, revising translations, adding and deleting footnotes, and giving each edition a fresh look, all in the attempt to make engaging with the Word of God easier and more enriching.

Consider the many people each Bible make-over requires—scholars, writers, editors, designers. With all those people involved, emails fly, documents are shared and altered, words are moved, and pages are laid out in new ways. The opportunities for errors sky-rocket. It can easily become the adult version of Telephone.

Finding and correcting the numerous potential errors can seem impossible. And for busy publishers and editors, it probably is. A dedicated proofreading process can help.

> 9 Seré paciente cuando el Señor me
>   castigue,
>   porque he pecado contra él.
> Pero después +él tomará mi caso
>   y me hará justicia por todo lo
>   que he sufrido a manos de mis
>   enemigos.
> El Señor me llevará a la luz
>   y veré su justicia.
> 10 Entonces mis enemigos verán que el

It is not unusual for us to find stray characters in Bibles we are proofreading even if they've been typeset by experienced typesetters.

Finding Hidden Errors

The sorts of mistakes proofreaders watch for are varied and run the gamut from missing text to wrong wording to general typos.

However, one quirky typo we see is one that is specific to the typesetting process and involves the software used.

Most Bibles are typeset in a program called Adobe InDesign. As with any software, InDesign's efforts to be helpful can sometimes create distractions for the reader, such as inserting bad line breaks or strange spacing issues. But consider this comment sent to one Bible publisher:

> **"My edition had a typo in Revelation 20:2 so that it read 'cWhains' instead of chains."**

This is not an isolated incident. Our proofreading team recently reviewed a Bible just before it went to print and found another mysterious *W*. Instead of referring to a mother hen, the verse spoke of a mother *when*.

So how in the world does a

> **37** O Jerusalem, Jerusalem, *thou* that killest the prophets, and stonest them which are sent unto thee, how often would I have gathered thy children together, even as a *when* gathereth her chickens under *her* wings, and ye would not!

typo like that get into the Bible? Typesetters and proofreaders know exactly how: an InDesign shortcut key. InDesign allows users to click Ctrl+W to view a page in a print-ready preview. It's a handy shortcut and used often. But there's a catch. If the wrong tool is selected, Ctrl+W will actually insert a *W* at the place of the cursor. In fact, a typesetter might not even realize it has happened, as the stray letter is easily absorbed into the more than 3,000 characters on a typical Bible page.

But for everyone who gets distracted by such flaws while trying to meet God in his Word, mistakes like these can seem huge. They matter.

Some of these errors may seem like no big deal. But for everyone who gets distracted by such flaws while trying to meet God in his Word, mistakes like these can seem huge. They matter.

Much like receiving a cup full of snakes instead of a cold, creamy shake.

Even the best Bible typesetters need a proofreader.

5

Bible Translation Distinctions

How different can they really be?

My new Bible is an NASB—that's what my preacher uses."

"I still read my childhood *Living Bible*; it feels like a warm hug."

"I only read literal translations of the Bible. I don't want translators interpreting anything for me."

"There's no debate here. We all know that Jesus spoke King James!"

If you have been in Bible publishing for any length of time, you have heard comments like these from readers.

Imagine you are buying your first Bible, one that you want to read and not just turn into shelf decor. You might visit a physical bookstore or an online retailer. Either way you shop, you are immediately confronted with shelves and shelves or screen after screen of beautiful designs, leather covers, embossed crosses, gold-edged paper, and a hodge-podge of letter combinations. You have no idea what CSB, KJV, NLT, ESV, NIrV, and NCV even mean, much less the differences between them.

You went shopping for your Bible thinking they were all about the same. But now you're not so sure.

Understand the Differences

For a Bible publisher, this scenario may be a distant memory. But if you are creating a new Bible project, it is important to understand some of these differences. It could be a costly mistake if you model your project in one translation after a project in a different translation without accounting for either one's design choices or editorial style.

But if you are creating a new Bible project, it is important to understand some of these differences.

Consider a situation in one of the Bible's history books. The New Living Translation (NLT) has 64 lines of poetry in 1 Chronicles. Great, a checklist! Something editors and proofers alike appreciate. But before you assume you've just found your heaven-inspired checklist and use it to check all your Bibles, note that in the New International Version (NIV), the poetry includes 80 lines, not 64, in the same book. This amounts to 16 lines that convey similar meanings but are represented with entirely different styles. (See other examples on page 28.)

It could be a costly mistake if you model your project in one translation after a project in a different translation without accounting for either one's design choices or editorial style.

Staying within the vein of the NLT and NIV comparisons, note that the NLT includes 186 cases of the small-capped LORD. Because this word convention is a translation of the Hebrew word *YHWH*, it should stand to reason that all the translations would match. But because of very valid and accurate translation differences, the NIV contains 176 small-capped *lords*—10 fewer than those in the NLT.

Although the message is the same, the translators found that they could accurately relate the Hebrew using slightly different sentences.

Even the names or spellings of some of the people found in the Bible can differ, such as the man who owned the threshing floor in 2 Chronicles 3:1. The NIV, NLT, and ICB (International Children's Bible) all refer to this man as Araunah. But the NKJV (New King James Version), KJV (King James Version), and ESV (English Standard Version) call him Ornan. But before you add this name to your checklist and conduct a global change in your project, it's worth noting that all six of these translations use Araunah for the same man in 2 Samuel 24:16.

IS IT ORNAN OR ARAUNAH?

Translations often spell the names of Bible Characters differently. Consider 2 Chronicles 3:1:

NIV	NKJV
"It was on the threshing floor of *Araunah* the Jebusite, the place provided by David."	". . . the place that David had prepared on the threshing floor of *Ornan* the Jebusite."

And is it Chedorlaomer we meet in Genesis 14:1 or Kedorlaomer? You may not know the answer, but you will certainly want your proofers to.

Beyond spelling differences, how a translation uses capital letters, hyphens, and spaces is something that should also give Bible editors pause. Take the name of the place cited in Joshua 9:17. It's called Kirjathjearim, Kiriath-jearim, and Kiriath Jearim across translations. And Genesis 4:22 calls a metal worker Tubalcain, Tubal-cain, and Tubal-Cain depending, again, on the translation.

How a translation uses capital letters, hyphens, and spaces is something that should also give Bible editors pause.

The Differences Go beyond Scripture

And for all that material that may surround the actual text of the Scripture, such as the preface, other front and back matter, sidebar features, and study notes, each publisher has a preferred way of referencing verses in their translation. From preferred book abbreviations to spacing to punctuation, there is a lot to keep track of; it's important to get your style guide right.

Is it confusing? Yes, but an experienced Bible proofreader will protect you from making a mistake because of the differences between Bible translations.

Investing in the right team of editors and proofreaders will save you the cost of reprint corrections later and copyright issues with a translation's owner.

6

Five Common Mistakes We Find When Proofreading a Bible

Here's a short list of everyday errors.

Remember that parable Jesus told about vinegar?

It's a trick question. He never told such a parable.

However, if your only Bible was the Authorized Version published in 1717 by John Baskett, you might not be so sure. Baskett's Bible accidentally titled Luke 20 "The Parable of the Vinegar" instead of "The Parable of the Vineyard." And, sadly, that wasn't its only flaw. Supposedly, people mocked this mistake-filled Bible project by calling it "a Baskett-ful of errors."

Ouch.

Every day our proofing team catches potentially giant blunders and also offers subtle

The parable of the vinegar.

S. Luke.

chief priests and the scribes came upon him, with the elders,

2 And spake unto him, saying, Tell us, By what authority doest thou these things? or who is he that gave thee this authority?

3 And he answered and said unto them, I will also ask you one thing; and answer me.

4 The Baptism of John, was it from heaven, or of men?

5 And they reasoned with themselves, saying, If we shall say, From heaven; he will say, Why then believed ye him not?

6 But and if we say, Of men; all the people will stone us: for they be perswaded that John was a prophet.

7 And they answered, that they could not tell whence *it was.*

8 And Jesus said unto them, Neither tell I you by what authority I do these things.

9 Then began he to speak to the people

scribes the
him; and
perceived
against th
20 A
forth spie
just men,
words, th
to the pe
nour.
21 An
fter, we
est rightl
son *of a*
||truly.
22 Is
to Cefar,
23 Bu
said unto
24 Sh
superscrip

The Vinegar Bible. Courtesy of Museum of the Bible Collection.
All rights reserved. Museum of the Bible 2020.

suggestions that will improve a reader's experience with the Bible.

Because we're dealing with God's Holy Word, we pay close attention to little things like fonts and spacing and footnotes. We work carefully to ensure that a publisher's design helps—not hinders—readers when it comes to engaging God's Word. Because even subtle imperfections can hinder readers from hearing God's voice through the Bible's pages, we do our best to eliminate any and all distractions.

Here are five of the most common mistakes we find in our Bible proofreading projects.

1. Unfortunate Word Breaks

When typesetting a Bible (or any book for that matter) according to the parameters of a specific layout/design, there's no way to avoid word breaks. Let's say, for example, you're nearing the end of a line, and the word *every-thing* won't fit. As a typesetter, you'd break the word, resulting in "every-" at the end of the line in question, and "thing" at the beginning of the next.

The word *everything* isn't so bad. But what if it's the word Nazirite? On the surface that seems easy enough, until you find Amazon reviews that lump your publishing company into

some crazy conspiracies because they alleged you intentionally broke the word as Nazi-rite. And not to devolve into fifth-grade-boy humor, but you can see where breaking the name Shittim (the place in Moab where the Israelites camped before entering Canaan) leads to an embarrassing result.

2. Running Heads

A running head is an indicator at the top of a page that tells a reader what's on that page. In Bibles, the running head typically shows the first and last verses on the two-page spread.

Imagine a new reader sitting in church with a new Bible. The pastor directs the congregation to turn to Psalm 27. If a running head hap-

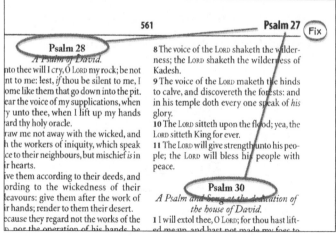

Incorrect running heads confuse, distract, and discourage readers.

pens to be erroneous, our once eager reader can end up on the wrong page and lose focus. The printed Bible that should have enhanced the pastor's sermon now becomes a distraction instead.

Although creating Bible running heads is often automated, we check and find incorrect running heads in almost every Bible we proofread.

Although creating Bible running heads is often automated, we check and find incorrect running heads in almost every Bible we proofread.

---

3. Missing Verses and Words

First Corinthians 6:9 (KJV) says, "Know ye not that the unrighteous shall not inherit the kingdom of God?" A Bible published in 1653 left out the second "not," thereby creating a scandal and earning the unflattering nickname The Unrighteous Bible.

Since "all Scripture" (literally "every word of Scripture") is inspired by God (2 Timothy 3:16), the last thing any publisher needs is to leave out a God-breathed word—or worse, an entire verse.

4. Misaligned Poetry

To most people, poetry alignment may not seem like a big deal, but consider one example from the GOD'S WORD Translation:

The correct layout of Psalm 23:1-3

The LORD is my shepherd.
    I am never in need.
        He makes me lie down in green pastures.
        He leads me beside peaceful waters.
        He renews my soul.

A wrong layout of Psalm 23:1-3

The LORD is my shepherd.
    I am never in need.
He makes me lie down in green pastures.
  He leads me beside peaceful waters.
    He renews my soul.

Poetry indents are translation decisions that establish primary and secondary thoughts.

The misalignment of the third line changes the emphasis of the first line. Rather than assuming a subordinate position (and highlighting the significance of the statement "I am never in need"), the phrase "He makes me lie down in green pastures" incorrectly becomes a primary and separate thought. Errant layouts can disrupt the reader's experience, distort the author's message, and destroy the beauty of Hebrew parallelism.

It's our conviction that the scholars of every translation made intentional choices regarding poetry layouts and poetry indentations that can affect the reading of the lines as much as the words themselves. Our mandate is to protect and preserve the translators' decisions as they worked hard at determining the inspired author's intent.

Errant layouts can disrupt the reader's experience, distort the author's message, and destroy the beauty of Hebrew parallelism.

---

5. Footnote Letters (Sigla) on the Wrong Page

Sigla (plural of *siglum*) are those small symbols used throughout biblical texts to alert readers to look in the margin for footnotes. These footnotes offer alternate translations or additional information useful for readers. Sigla are quite common in Bible projects.

Here's a list of modern translations and the approximate number of textual footnotes in each:

- NIV 3,300
- CSB 7,200
- NLT 4,750
- NKJV 3,000
- NRSV 3,000
- ESV 3,800
- NTV 4,750

While those are big numbers, the simple checking process is never straightforward.

8 For the choir director: A psalm of David, to be accompanied by a stringed instrument.*

¹O LORD, our Lord, your majestic name fills the earth!
Your glory is higher than the heavens.
²You have taught children and infants
to tell of your strength,*
silencing your enemies
and all who oppose you.

*Translation Notes 7:12 Hebrew he. 8:TITLE Hebrew according to the gittith. 8:2 Greek version reads to give you praise. Compare Matt 21:16.

Examples of footnotes. Bible proofreading ensures each siglum and footnote are on the correct page.

Some translations dedupe dozens of footnotes in any specific edition. This occurs when identical footnotes at the bottom of the page are combined so that multiple footnote markers in the Bible text point to the same footnote at the bottom of the page. Some translations do this a few hundred times, but knowing when to do so requires a strict adherence to following the translator's rules.

Occasionally in the process of typesetting, sigla—and the verses they shed light on—can end up on wrong pages. This isn't catastrophic, of course, but it is frustrating for readers and can disrupt an otherwise meaningful, devotional reading of God's Word.

Occasionally in the process of typesetting, sigla—and the verses they shed light on—can end up on wrong pages. This isn't catastrophic, of course, but it is frustrating for readers and can disrupt an otherwise meaningful, devotional reading of God's Word.

Jesus never told any parables about vinegar. He did, however, urge his followers on a number of occasions to "be careful." In our view, nowhere is that command more important than in the handling, proofing, and printing of the very message of God as printed in his Word.

God's Word deserves to
be presented perfectly.

7

Digital and Human: The Hybrid Proofing Approach

Relying on only electronic or human checks
will offer an incomplete review.

Almost anyone who spent time in front of a television set in the 1970s remembers the hit series the *Six Million Dollar Man*. You can probably still see Colonel Steve Austin's eyes as he realizes his NASA test flight is failing. You may still picture his ship crashing to the earth. Can you hear the narrator? "We can rebuild him. We have the technology. We have the capability to make the world's first bionic man."

By the end of the opening credits, Austin has been rebuilt with several bionic body parts. He can now run sixty miles an hour. He's got telescopic vision. And he's strong enough to take down any criminal and send him flying into the nearest police station. He has become a cyborg—part man, part machine. He is now "better than he was before. Better. Stronger. Faster."

And all for a measly $6 million.

In its heyday, the *Six Million Dollar Man* was outlandish, campy fun. But more than four decades later, technology has managed to move many crazy ideas from the realm of science fiction into scientific reality. Stunning advancements in robotics, computer technology, automation, and artificial intelligence (AI) are radically changing how the world works.

Very quickly, we can verify that the Bible text is complete: every verse is present and every paragraph is accounted for.

This is true even in Bible publishing. At Peachtree, we depend more and more on advancing technology to help us deliver Bible projects that are both beautiful and error-free.

Don't misunderstand. No one on our staff is bionic. We've never hired a cyborg (that we know of). But we do take advantage of the best and latest technology, even as our team continues to offer wise judgment on every page of every project.

We're convinced that modern Bible publishing requires the latest digital tools and the best human expertise. We rely on both.

The Role of "Machines"

When we onboard a new project from a client, we use proprietary, custom-built software programs to do what only they can do. They're fast and highly reliable. Very quickly, we can verify that the Bible text is complete: every verse is present and every paragraph is accounted for.

We're convinced that modern Bible publishing requires the latest digital tools and the best human expertise. We rely on both.

We further use our advanced digital tools to search for specific problem areas and to ensure that passages are presented correctly. When we discover a unique problem, we can create a custom search tool to identify and locate other places in a project where that same problem might occur.

If, for example, the siglum (plural *sigla*)—that tiny symbol that points to a footnote or marginal note—is too close to the chapter number, we can quickly develop and run a search that locates other places where this occurs. Advanced tools like these not only save time and increase accuracy but also relieve the stress of wondering if we've found all the occurrences of a problem.

The Role of Humans

Electronic tools make great servants but poor masters. They're incredibly helpful, but on their own they're incomplete. Computers still cannot read with a human's discernment. If a space between words is too great or too small or just doesn't "feel" right, a computer can't tell you that.

Electronic tools make great servants but poor masters. They're incredibly helpful, but on their own they're incomplete.

And consider an electronic tool as simple as spell-check. This resource has amazing power and can save its users much embarrassment.

But if you rely solely on spell-check and fail to pass a human eye over the same text, you could end up with quite a few mistakes. Spell-check doesn't catch homophones (words that are pronounced the same but are spelled differently). Consider an example:

> **"Four God sew loved the whirled that He gave his only begotten sun that whomever believes in hymn should knot parish but have eternal life."**
> **Jon 316**

That nonsensical sentence will pass your spell-check program, but it will also earn you plenty of one-star reviews.

Our Hybrid Scripture Integrity Program

While the world's best Bible typesetters have character-for-character tools that can verify the Bible text, these tools are not foolproof. They're only as good as the operators using them. Mistakes can (and do) still slip through even the most sophisticated comparison programs.

Some of the things these programs cannot catch:

- The spacing between words
- The correct location of running heads
- The proper placement of text boxes on each page

For this reason, Bible typesetting and proof-reading is best done with a hybrid proofing approach: humans and machines. We find our electronic tools sync well with (a) the rigorous checks our experienced Scripture Integrity Team uses and (b) the electronic checks employed by the typesetters.

We find our electronic tools sync well with (a) the rigorous checks our experienced Scripture Integrity Team uses and (b) the electronic checks employed by the typesetters.

The Human Element at Work

Our team still prints out every page of most Bible projects. We study each page intently, checking even the distribution of ink on paper. Research suggests that the human eye is more forgiving toward text on screens than on paper. So proofreaders who rely solely on what they can see on a computer screen often miss things that can only be seen on a physical page.

Our approach is to let computers be computers and let readers be readers. By having our skilled team work in tandem with the latest and most effective proofing technologies, we're best able to hit our target: producing perfect Bibles.

By having our skilled team work in tandem with the latest and most effective proofing technologies, we're best able to hit our target: producing perfect Bibles.

To the outside observer, our offices may not look as exciting as the world of the *Six Million Dollar Man*. But we Bible proofers are Word nerds through and through, and we think this life is pretty exciting.

The best Bible proofing is a hybrid of computer and human effort.

8

The End of the Line: Fussing Over Word Breaks and Stacks

Caution: word br-

eaks ahead.

A piece of equipment breaks down. An order breaks during shipment. A manager starts taking two-hour lunch breaks. What else is there to say? In a broken world, breaks are a pesky part of business.

In Bible publishing, editors, designers, and typesetters wrestle with two other kinds of breaks: word breaks and stacks. Both can be distracting, and both keep us busy.

Word breaks are how we make lines of text fit into an allotted space and make them easier to read. Without appropriate word breaks, text can end up either crammed too tightly together or spaced too far apart. When word breaks are used carelessly, they become a hindrance. When deployed indiscriminately, they're like jarring, irritating potholes in a reader's journey through the Bible.

We recently proofed a Bible that had 500 word breaks in Genesis. Five hundred! Over the course of 832 pages, that Bible had 8,762 word breaks. That sounds like a lot, but it's fairly typical.

And we check word breaks in every Bible we work on. So, what really is the problem?

Bad Word Breaks Are Distracting

The goal of a new Bible project is to get people to engage with the One the Word reveals, so anything that gets in the way of that divine encounter is a problem. Imagine a reader getting swept up in the truth and power of a passage but then getting tripped up as he or she must stop to make sense of a clumsy word break. Even momentary disruptions in reading can hinder deeper understanding.

Bible text with loving-kindness broken incorrectly. This incorrect break is a very common suggestion by InDesign and would be printed if left unchecked.

We do everything in our power to avoid word breaks that divert a reader's focus—even for a moment.

Bad Word Breaks Are Confusing

What's worse than a distracting word break? A confusing one.

Over the course of 832 pages, that Bible had 8,762 word breaks. That sounds like a lot, but it's fairly typical.

Layout programs are designed to automatically insert word breaks—for our convenience. But in our experience, these programs are wrong far too often. Technology might be getting smarter and better, but some things still need human intervention.

Consider the word *present*. You're at the end of a line and the entire word won't fit. Do you break it as "pre-sent" or "pres-ent"?

It depends. The word gets broken differently, depending on whether it's a noun, a verb, or an adjective. Even though the average reader isn't a professional editor, our brains know that *pre-sent* is a verb (the act of offering someone something), and the stress is on the second syllable. The word *pres-ent* can be a noun (the thing that is given) or an adjective (meaning to be at hand). Break the word in the wrong place and you'll confuse the reader. (In addition to the word *present*, other words present a similar challenge: *attribute*, *project*, *rebel*, *refuse*—and the list goes on.)

As the saying goes, if you confuse the reader, you'll lose the reader. That's why a good typesetter takes care to limit unnecessary word breaks. But when they can't be avoided, we make sure they don't muddy the message of a text.

Bad Word Breaks Are Disturbing

Leave your page design software in charge of breaking words at the ends of lines and certain biblical words—think Nazirite and Shittim—can get divided in an unfortunate way. The result can leave sixth-grade boys snickering and elbowing one another and adults shaking their heads. And even without the snickers, do you really want Jesus's "demon-stration" of God's power to read, "Jesus's demon-"?

That's the last thing anyone wants—time with God derailed by unnecessary, intrusive thoughts and a devotional time hijacked by words that don't belong.

Stacks Can Be a Problem Too

While our team is double-checking all those word breaks, we also check stacks. Stacks are what editors and designers call consecutive lines that begin or end with the same word, word ending, or punctuation mark.

Like word breaks, stacks present a typesetting dilemma. They pose a visual challenge and can even play tricks on a reader. Instead of reading effortlessly from one line to the next, your eye can skip a line, or even two, when there's a stack of the same word or phrase.

Here's an example:

out the blood at the base   He came down
[10] He burned the fat, the   sin offering, the
d the fatty lobe of the   he fellowship
the sin offering on the   and Aaron the
LORD had commanded   of meeting. W

It can happen at the beginning of a line too:

fering with them is to be of fine
flour mixed with oil; offer six
quarts with each bull and four
quarts with the ram. [21] Offer two
quarts with each of the seven
lambs [22] and one male goat for a
sin offering to make atonement

Like bad word breaks, stacks can also cause confusion. Stacks require readers to break their train of thought, back up, and reread. Suddenly the reader is no longer in the text experiencing it but outside of it, trying to make sense of the words.

Rereading is not the end of the world, of course. However, stacks are just another distraction that can frustrate readers. They can also contribute to that diabolical whisper so many Bible readers hear in their minds: "See how complicated this ancient book is? All these tiny, strange words on all these thin pages—I'll never understand it!"

A two-column Bible produces about 115,000 lines of Bible text, with the potential for stacks to appear at either side—left-hand or right-hand—of each column. Between stacks and word breaks, our team must check over a quarter of a million places where these could occur.

A two-column Bible produces about 115,000 lines of Bible text, with the potential for stacks to appear at either side—left-hand or right-hand—of each column.

Why do we check so closely? Because God's Word is worth it. We don't want any reader anywhere closing God's Word and breaking early.

Bad word breaks are distracting and confusing and can even be disturbing.

9

Many Will Call Him lord . . . Lord . . . Lord

Which one, Lord?

Do you remember the story in Genesis when three men, one being God in the flesh, appeared to the elderly Abraham and told him his wife would have a son within the year? Although Sarah was a decade younger than Abraham, she was equally elderly and had been barren all her life. Sarah overheard the pronouncement and laughed at the prospect.

Genesis 18:12–14 says:

Therefore Sarah laughed within herself, saying, After I am waxed old shall I have pleasure, my *lord* being old also? And the Lord said unto Abraham, Wherefore did Sarah laugh, saying, Shall I of a surety bear a child, which am old? Is any thing too hard for the Lord? At the time appointed I will return unto thee, according to the time of life, and Sarah shall have a son (KJV, emphasis added).

Regardless of the 500 years between now and the time this was translated—and aside from the phrases such as "waxed old," "of a surety," and "unto thee"—this passage is fairly easy to understand.

But why are some occasions of the word *Lord* capped and others not? This small difference points to a huge distinction.

Do All Lords Lead to God?

You may have noticed in your own Bible reading (and in the italic words in the passage above), that the simple four-letter word *lord* is capitalized differently throughout the Bible. If a person doesn't understand the purpose of these differences, he may think all instances of this word point to God. And because the capitalized *L* and "small caps" *ord* (LORD) looks "formal," it must simply be a symbol of honor. Formal means honor, right?

This capitalization style, though, has great meaning. The use of no caps versus small caps (or all caps) means the difference between an earthly master or a husband and the God of the universe. That's a big difference.

Without the differentiation between a man and a specific name for God, this passage could be misunderstood to mean:

> After I am waxed old . . . God being old
> also? And the man of the house said to
> Abraham . . . is anything too hard for
> the master?

But why are some occasions of the word Lord *capped and others not? This small difference points to a huge distinction.*

Not only does this sound strange, but it is extremely inaccurate. By getting the *lords* mixed up, we would be calling God old and relegating him to the man of the house. But we know God is both ageless and the Creator of all men . . . and houses. It is imperative that we get this right.

So what does it all mean, and how can we be sure that the Bibles we produce are accurate?

In most English Bibles, when the word *lord* appears in small caps (LORD) or all caps (LORD), it refers to the Hebrew word *YHWH*, a most holy name for God that originally contained no vowels and meant "to be." You will recognize this meaning when recalling the voice of God coming from the burning bush and telling Moses that his name was "I AM" (Exodus 3:14). In English Bibles, it is sometimes translated as Jehovah or Yahweh.

When other names for God are used, such as the Hebrew word *Adonai*, the English word *Lord* is represented with uppercase and lowercase letters just as any name would be.

Over 6,000 Chances for Error

Consider this: there are over 6,000 occurrences of the small cap *Lord* in English and Spanish Bibles. Getting the *lords* wrong can change the meaning tremendously. Sometimes inexperienced editors or typesetters see that the word *Lord* is most often represented with small caps and, to save time, may make the mistake of doing a global "fix," changing all instances of the word to small caps.

This global change represents a huge problem for the typesetter, as each wrong instance must be changed back. And while our Scripture Integrity Team rarely sees this type of global problem in a Bible project, it's not unusual to find several stray capitalization mistakes. Of course, finding that one stray mistake—one that easily slips through spell-check—means staying vigilant over the thousands of occasions of the word.

There are over 6,000 occurrences of the small cap Lord *in English and Spanish Bibles.*

Getting these titles and names right matters. Mistakes in how these four little letters are capitalized could be the equivalent of removing God from a verse entirely. Ensure the proofreading team you entrust your Bible project to knows how to spot the correct formatting of each *Lord*.

The difference between lord *and* Lord *couldn't possibly be larger.*

10

Nine Common Errors We Find in Specialty Bible Projects

We routinely find repeated mistakes while proofing devotional and study Bibles.

The next time you visit a bookstore, take a moment to marvel at the multitude of available study and devotional Bibles. You might want to tip your cap to "Bloody Mary," the Catholic queen of England in the 1550s. She's indirectly responsible for all those helpful Bibles.

Under Mary's violent reign, prominent British Protestants fled to the European continent. One group of Reformation scholars hunkered down in Geneva and decided to make the most of their exile. They launched an ambitious project to give William Tyndale's New Testament a complete makeover.

The result in 1560 was the Geneva Bible. Talk about "new and improved"! This version of God's Word was more readable and affordable. It was also more compact, even though it contained a wealth of extra helps for readers. Never before had a Bible contained maps, indexes, cross-references, chapter divisions, numbered verses, and explanatory marginal notes.

In short, all those popular study and devotional Bibles used by contemporary believers—for example, the *Thompson Chain-Reference Bible*, the *Life Application Study Bible*, the *ESV* and *NIV Study Bibles*—can trace their heritage back to the venerable Geneva Bible.

Each additional note or feature, each map and chart contains the possibility of human error.

Study Bibles offer not only God's Holy Word but a wealth of information and encouragement for those who want to better understand and live out their faith. And yet all that ancillary content represents a challenge for Bible publishers. Each additional note or feature, each map and chart contains the possibility of human error. That's why every specialty Bible project should be carefully proofread before printing.

Here are the nine common errors we catch when proofreading study and devotional Bibles:

1. Typos

"There is now condemnation for those who are in Christ Jesus."

Did you catch the missing word? It's no small mistake. Romans 8:1 says, "There is now *no* condemnation . . ." (emphasis added). This is an actual example of a study note that appeared under the Bible text in a project we were proofing. Uncaught and uncorrected, this sentence would have given the opposite meaning of what God said and what an editor meant to convey.

Since study notes don't benefit from the years of proofing that the Bible text gets, it's easy for an error like this to slip through. Thus, the necessity of checking every word carefully, using the *Chicago Manual of Style* and vigilant editorial care to ensure the delivery of an excellent product.

2. Wrong wording

This often happens when a study Bible is translated from one version to another (e.g., KJV to NIV). A study note may reference the previous translation—an understandable editorial mistake, but one that is confusing and potentially discouraging to the reader. Here's a practical example, which includes Isaiah 7:15 in three different, excellent translations. A study note that is translated from one translation to another will need to be thoughtfully edited. While the meaning of the verse doesn't change, the words used in the study note will likely need to be updated:

KJV	NIV	NLT
Butter and honey shall he eat, that he may know to refuse the evil, and choose the good.	He will be eating curds and honey when he knows enough to reject the wrong and choose the right.	By the time this child is old enough to choose what is right and reject what is wrong, he will be eating yogurt and honey.

3. The wrong reference or cross-reference

How many times have you looked up a cited reference or cross-reference and said to yourself, "I'm sure there must be a connection here, but I don't see it"? Rather than grasp the message of God's undying and caring love, the reader might leave the note concluding *I knew it . . . I'm not smart enough to understand the Bible.* The editor may have saved time by not proofing each reference, but the choice can have unwanted consequences.

4. Notes on the wrong page

The benefit of Bible study notes is that they can live alongside the verse/verses they explain. But when they get separated from their accompanying verse/verses and end up on a different page, it's a hassle for the reader. When that happens, the hard work that went into a study note can be wasted because the note isn't usually read. Again the goal in proofing and laying out a Bible is to facilitate ease of use, avoid confusion, and eliminate all possible distractions.

5. Formatting mistakes

Are certain words supposed to be in italics? In bold? In quotation marks? What if the wrong font is introduced or a layout is inconsistent? Sloppy formatting errors like these undermine the value of God's Word.

22:18 KILLED .. EIGHTY-FIVE PRIESTS. God _Bold_
allowed Doeg to kill God's ministers and other innocent men, women and children. In a sinful world, where people have chosen to defy God and go their own way, evil and destruction are normal occurrences. When this happens, innocent people sometimes suffer unjustly. God's people should

6. Incomplete text

Occasionally in all that great ancillary material, the end of a sentence or paragraph gets deleted or somehow ends up missing. The reader was starting to gain a new insight, but suddenly the note

(See what we mean?)

7. Covering up the Bible text

Sometimes a helpful note or map looks really good, until you realize it's covering up the biblical text. A designer or typesetter inadvertently overlaid the Bible text. Even though the text is present, it's actually hidden, invisible to the reader. This may sound crazy, but it happens in layouts more often than you'd think.

9 Behold, I will make them of the synagogue of Satan, which say they are Jews, and are not, but do lie; behold, I will make them to come and worship before thy feet, and to know that I have loved thee.
10 Because thou hast kept the word of my patience, I also will keep thee from the hour of temptation, which shall come upon all the world, to try them that dwell upon the earth.

22 He that hath an ear, let him hear what the Spirit saith unto the churches.

8. Inconsistent style

Is the proper term the Feast of the Passover, the Feast of Unleavened Bread, or just Passover? Is it the Feast of Tabernacles, Festival of Booths, Sukkot, or Feast of Ingathering? Is it Abimelech or Abimelek? Is that two different people or the same person with an accidental, different spelling? Consistency in names is one of the many simple ways we can help the reader. Consistent use helps readers track along and get the main point of an explanatory note while not getting lost trying to connect dots.

9. Improper use of *Lord*

"The LORD said to my Lord ..."

Setting "ORD" in small caps in "LORD" is used to denote the Hebrew word *Yahweh*. When small caps are not preserved, the meaning of the word is completely changed. (See chapter 9.)

Every Bible project has more than 300,000 details to get right. A thorough proofreading of the Bible will check them all.

The point of all the extra features in a devotional or study Bible is to aid the reader in understanding the truth of God, not to confuse him or her. That's why proofreaders go the extra mile. Every Bible project has more than 300,000 details to get right. A thorough proofreading of the Bible will check them all.

We believe readers deserve Bibles that are free of distracting errors. Most importantly, God deserves our best effort in transmitting his Word to the next generation of readers.

11

Why You Need a Specialist

Bible proofreading is a three-phase process.

If you thought you had a serious health condition, you wouldn't turn to the SpeedyCare clinic on the corner, even if the people there are really nice. You'd make an appointment with your trusted doctor. In all likelihood, he or she would run a few tests and refer you to a specialist—a neurologist, a cardiologist, or another *-ologist*.

This is the world we live in. Everything is specialized. People become experts, not just in a field, but in one particular facet of a field. This is not a bad thing; there's just so much to know. No one can adequately master all the knowledge and skills needed to do *every*thing.

Publishing is highly specialized too. Just because an editor is in demand when it comes to whipping inspirational fiction manuscripts into shape doesn't mean she is equipped or trained to tackle the complexities of a massive Bible project.

We speak from experience. Bible editorial work is the skill we've been mastering for nearly forty years. When you've got a Bible publishing project, you want it done with excellence. And we do too.

When you've got a Bible publishing project, you want it done with excellence.

What are best practices for Bible proofreading? The road map for success follows the same path we've developed over the years and includes a three-phase process.

Peachtree's Three-Phase Process

Step One: Project Onboarding

You probably know what will happen to a long-distance trip if the navigator is even a fraction of a degree off course. If his miscalculation is caught early, it will take little effort to get back on track. But the more time that goes by without a correction, the farther the navigator ends up from his destination.

In a similar way, the sooner little errors are caught in a Bible layout the better, preventing huge, expensive problems later. Case in point: Genesis represents the first 4.9 percent of the Bible. When we catch systematic errors there, we can stop them before they have a chance to grow. Can you imagine what a seemingly small error in Genesis would look like once it reached Isaiah?

The sooner little errors are caught in a Bible layout the better, preventing huge, expensive problems later.

In this first stage, we pore over an initial test file and examine it for small issues that can turn into big problems. Specifically, we look to see if Bible verses are missing, if notes are on the correct page, if paragraphs and special settings are set correctly. Asking the typesetter to reset even one paragraph or list could potentially reflow dozens of pages. That's why we want to find and fix such things early—to save you time and help preserve your budget so you can use those funds to distribute your newly printed Bible.

Step Two: Scripture Integrity Check

Step two is where we begin a line-by-line review of the Bible pages. Four or five team members look at each page and check each line of Scripture. (That's a *lot* of looking, since each Bible usually has more than 100,000 lines.) Our team checks and double-checks footnotes and cross-references. We run custom software we've developed to ensure every bit of the Bible is intact. We also look at ancillary content—study notes, special features, and the like.

We examine every line of every project to ensure every copyright requirement is met and every word is accounted for.

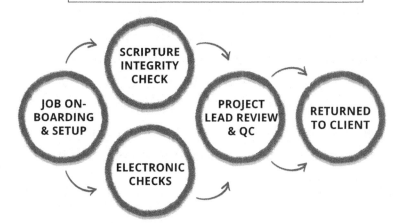

PROJECT LEAD OVERSIGHT

SCRIPTURE INTEGRITY CHECK

JOB ON-BOARDING & SETUP

PROJECT LEAD REVIEW & QC

RETURNED TO CLIENT

ELECTRONIC CHECKS

Step Three: Project Lead Review

In step three of our quality control process, all high-visibility items (e.g., running heads, chapter starts, page numbers, etc.) are double-checked. The project lead collates the work of the Scripture Integrity Team members. And then, all notes and comments are routed back to the publisher, editor, or typesetter and presented in the way that we have agreed upon at the start of the project.

We examine every line of every project to ensure every copyright requirement is met and every word is accounted for.

This is the meticulous process we've followed over a thousand times. While there are many motivations in publishing, our drive is from the heart: we aim to make sure each new Bible project we deliver allows the Spirit of God to work powerfully (Hebrews 4:12)—without the distraction of human errors.

Experience matters because there is too much that can go wrong in Bible publishing.

12

The Kind of Publicity You Don't Want

*Skipping a proofread can cost
three or four stars.*

P. T. Barnum, the flamboyant showman of the nineteenth century, famously said, "All publicity is good publicity."

Perhaps all publicity is good publicity for the person who's famous for being famous. Any day that a spotlight-seeking celebrity gets to push past the paparazzi's cameras, bask in an overflow of attention, and get fingers tweeting is a good day.

Maybe we should finish the quote attributed to P. T. Barnum: "All publicity is good publicity as long as they spell your name right." That sounds a lot like Barnum was stressing the importance of proofreading.

In the world of Bible publishing, perhaps not *all* publicity is good publicity. If the goal of a person or business is to simply become famous (or infamous), Barnum was right: any publicity will do. But if the goal is business success, you want *positive* publicity. You want good buzz, positive word-of-mouth. You want consumers praising your products. In today's world that means you want five-star reviews.

The fact is, consumers read reviews. You probably do too. You may have even done it this week. You visited your favorite online retailer, the one that has your favorites list, shipping address, and credit card on file. You found your must-have product. You looked at the price and then scrolled down to the reviews section. That make-or-break-a-sale section. What are people saying about your item? The answers can cause you to add the item to your cart or move on to a different product.

The fact is, consumers read reviews.

This process is no different for people shopping for a new Bible.

One of the most powerful ways to spread the word about your Bible project is through these product reviews. Four- and five-star reviews can help drive distribution. But a Bible with consistently low ratings will just become stored inventory. The publisher loses out on the sales and ministry it might otherwise have had.

Imagine investing months and months of your time and labor editing a Bible project. Imagine your joy at seeing it roll off the press. And now imagine the horror you'd feel if you read an Amazon review like this one.

All was well until one day, from the pulpit, I had trouble finding Isaiah 65. Though still somewhat useful, I would rather not have four books with significant problems (It goes like this: pages 1-288, followed by 225-256, then 321-799, so I am missing 289-320)! So, if you buy, check the pages and return. Don't wait to discover the problem like I did . . . in front of my whole congregation!

Is this a typesetting problem or a printing problem? We've seen pagination issues like this land in both places. In fact, for a Bible with these problems, three stars is quite generous. But any shopper reading the review itself will certainly move on to another Bible—or not buy a Bible at all.

This project now becomes cases of Bibles that can't be distributed.

It helps to know that every Bible project is

going to involve errors during development and typesetting. It also helps to know that those mistakes will be found by someone. They can be found by a trained proofreading team *before* the Bible goes to press or by alert readers *after* it's been published. The former is a private affair, between the publishing and proofreading team. The latter? Well, you can see just how public this becomes by looking at the online reviews we've reprinted below.

(Note that we removed the names of the Bible product and publisher from the following reviews. However, we are happy to say that none of the negative reviews were for projects proofed by Peachtree's Scripture Integrity Team.)

... disgusted that anyone publishing a bible would leave a whole sentence out. Wow.

In Genesis 3:8, the word "among" is missing and in the book of Psalms a "t" is missing from the word "brought.". . . I will read the whole Bible and note them so that I can call the publisher and let them know.

I have been enjoying this . . . Bible for a while. However, today I found a typo in this Bible. In Isaiah 58:8, the last word should be "rereward" (= rearward), NOT "reward" Other than the typo, this is a good KJV study Bible on the market.

The QUALITY is disappointing. . . . I have found so many typos and printing errors as I am reading. Words misspelled or words printed with no space between them. I am not a high-detail person, but this has bothered me so much. I'm still using it, but it's frustrating. . . . I had got this Bible to use for a while and then give to one of my kids, and the content is great. I have no complaints about it, but the printing quality is terrible and I'd be embarrassed to give it to them.

I have found several mistakes in the printing of my . . . Bible and I have not even completed reading all 66 books of the Bible yet. Three errors to date.

Amos 5:20 is printed "shall not tne day of"

Joshua 19:10 the word "was" is incorrect (struck over)

1 Samuel 21:8 there is an extra period between the words neither and brought

The reviews that appear in this chapter have been excerpted and adapted from Amazon.com and Christianbook.com.

Some think, "With 31,000+ verses in the Bible, is a single typo really a big deal?"

Consider the following review from Christianbook.com:

> As far as early impressions go, there is a typo in the PREFACE which doesn't exactly fill me with confidence. . . . Just 'one' letter has lost my confidence. . . . It may not be much, but it is everything; how something like this could escape the eyes of editors and proofreaders etc., especially in a work of this importance and nature . . . If the explanation is a typo, one may as well throw it in the bin. This I sadly rate with negative 1 star. Personally, credibility is tarnished from the outset, the worst place to lose your reader, and regrettably, I am forced by editorial haphazardness to consider this work as merely just another translation. This may be harsh, but I have no desire to do the work of the editor or proofreader.

Ouch.

When our team reviews a Bible, we ask to see front and back matter as well. Those pages are typically put together quickly and usually at the last minute, which makes it easy to miss errors. The following review is from a Bible that we *did* proofread. Unfortunately, the editor never sent us the presentation page. A single typo on that highly visible page cost this publisher two stars:

This is a lovely Bible but there's a typo on the presentation page! . . . Happy to keep it as it's just for me but wanted to mention it in case people buy it for a gift.

People read and rate Bibles differently than they do fiction or nonfiction books, where typos are inconvenient but acceptable. When there are typos or other errors in a Bible, readers often return it, seeing it as defective. We all believe God's Word is perfect. It's difficult to accept that the publishers of Bibles are not.

People read and rate Bibles differently than they do fiction or nonfiction books.

A reliable Bible proofreader will help protect you from costly mistakes. With a good process, reviews like this one can be more of the norm.

I love this Bible! It is so readable...and I love it. Thanks so much!

And this one:

> ...I decided to go with this one. When it arrived, I checked it. ... Now, two more tests: how it holds up to daily use and whether there are any typos or omissions- the sort of things it could take a while to spot. If I find anything, I will up-date this review. So far though, I will say this is a beautiful bible with lots of helpful study aids. ...

"All publicity is good publicity"? Not when you're in the Bible business. Obviously P. T. Barnum did not live in the always-connected, always-vocal online world.

Proofreading helps avoid the pain of bad reviews.

APPENDIX

Peachtree's Bible Proofreading Terms

AA: This means "Author's Alteration/Adjustment." It refers to any changes the translators or copyright holder have made to the text since its original release. Bible proofreaders must keep up with these changes and ensure they are included in new editions. These are also called errata.

Abut: Proofing term for when two letters or characters are touching and should not be.

Align: This is typically used to mark when multiple lines in a special setting or poetry do not align with each other. It may also refer to columns that are not aligned.

Arabic Numerals: These are the type of numbers commonly used in the US: 1, 2, 3, etc. As opposed to Roman numerals, which are letters representing numbers: I, II, III, i, v, x, etc.

Ascender: Part of a character or lowercase

letter that ascends above the base line. So "h" has an ascender.

Back Matter: Material following the main text, such as articles, a bibliography, a glossary, an index, a concordance, and maps. These pages are numbered in Arabic numerals. Also called end matter.

Base Line: This is the line that the main part of the letters "sit on." Ascenders go up and descenders go down from it. When checking line spacing, we measure from base line to base line.

Better Break: See Preferred Breaks.

Bf: A shorthand symbol that means to change the text to a boldface font.

Bible Book Numbers: The numerical order of the books of the Bible, always using a two-digit number. Genesis is 01 and Revelation is 66. Front matter is numbered 00 and back or end matter is 67 and up. See chart on page 120.

Block: Most often used at chapter starts to indicate that two, three, or four lines by the chapter number are aligned in a special way. We mark in the margins with "block."

Blues: These are a set of proofs that come

from the printer, showing the pages as they are laid out on the press. They should be checked against the final proofs.

Callout: In footnotes or cross-references it is the chapter and verse numbers (e.g., 23:4). In study notes it can be just a chapter:verse or also the words repeated directly from the Scripture text.

Caret: A proofreading mark ^ that looks like an upside down "V" and is used in the text to indicate where a correction needs to be made. Sometimes we use a superscript right-side-up "V" to insert quote marks or a fn/c.r. siglum.

Castoff: A typesetter's estimate of how many pages the Bible will be.

Chapter Starts/Blocks: Some Bibles have "drop numbers" and some have "drop letters/caps" to begin chapters in the Bible. There are usually two lines of text, or one line and a line space, making up the chapter block. Some projects may have a three- or four-line chapter block. When checking these, be sure that the numbers/letters are the same size and font and that there is consistent space between the number/letter and the text. Also check that the text alignment matches the translation style/

rules. Some translations have "run-in chapter starts" where there is no paragraph break between the end of one chapter and the start of the next. Each translation will have rules for how this is done. In one-chapter books and the Psalms the first letter of verse I is often used as the chapter start instead of a chapter or psalm number.

Character: A character is any letter, number, or punctuation symbol.

Chiasm: A chiasm is a repetition of similar ideas in the reverse sequence. Chiasms are structured in a repeating A-B-C ... C'-B'-A' pattern. For example, Jesus's words in Mark 2:27 are in the form of a chiasm: "The Sabbath was made for man, not man for the Sabbath." Using the ABB'A' form, the words *Sabbath* and *man* are repeated in reverse order. (The term *chiasm* comes from the Greek letter *chi*, which looks like our letter *X*.)

Clean Pages: Pages without marks. Contrast with fouled pages.

CMS/*Chicago Manual of Style*: The reference book that many publishers use for style guidelines. The most current one is the 17th edition. A few publishers still use the 16th edition.

Colophon: A short, printed notice, usually at or near the end of the book, where the publisher gives details of the book's production, such as the editorial team, the typesetter, the proofreader, its typeface, etc.

Columns: Abbreviate "col" or "cols." Scripture columns must usually align at the top and bottom.

Copy: This is a copy of a Bible or database that serves as the authority when checking new proofs. All settings and indents of new Bibles should match this master copy.

Cross-references: Abbreviate "ref" or "c.r." These are passages that refer to similar thoughts or events or that have the same word(s) as the text.

CWMS/*Christian Writer's Manual of Style***:** This is currently in the 4th edition. It is used by many publishers—either before or after consulting CMS.

Database: The database contains all the words and numbers that are in the text, footnotes, and cross-references. Also included are the codes telling the typesetting program if something is a paragraph, poetry, bold, a small cap, a superscript, or another setting.

Dedupe: When two or more footnotes on the same page (or in the same verse if applicable) have *identical* information. *Dedupe* is a shortened phrase for "delete duplicate." If footnotes dedupe in a particular translation, it means

- the footnote text is only printed once on the page.
- the same letter/number/symbol is used in the Scripture for that footnote in every location on the page.
- at the bottom of the page any verse number (or ch:v, depending on the translation) where that fn appeared should be included at the beginning of the fn, in the order of its appearance.

Descender: The part of a lowercase letter or character that "descends" below the base line. A "g" has a descender.

Diacritical Marks: These are marks for pronunciation used in some KJV databases. They include hyphens for syllables and accent marks. When a project is using these, we always accept those word breaks even if they don't match our list (for example, Lá-hai–roi where the en dash represents a hard hyphen in the word). Diacritics are also the markings used on some foreign language words. Example: mañana (tilde over the "n").

Drop Cap: This is when the first letter of the chapter is used in place of a chapter number. If the chapter starts with quotation marks, they should not be the size of the drop cap. Per CMS 13.37 the quotation marks should either match the size of the normal text or be dropped altogether.

Ellipses (pl.)/Ellipsis: Ellipses are used when words are intentionally missing from the text. There are two styles of ellipses. The first is created as a symbol in a Word document (…). There are no spaces between the dots, and the dots become a single character. The second is created by actually typing periods and spaces (. . . ; we mark as #.#.#.#). Whichever style is chosen by the publisher must be consistent throughout the project. There should be equal space on both sides of the ellipsis. The symbol will not break at the end of a line, but the space/dot ellipsis will. When checking word breaks, be sure that all three dots are on the same line.

End Matter: See Back Matter.

First Pages: The initial set of PDFs created by the typesetter usually have this name. The second round of pages is called second pages, and so forth.

Flush Left: Align at the left margin for the setting (f.l.).

Flush Right: Align at the right margin for the setting (f.r.).

Folio: Another word for page number.

Font: The typeface used for the text. It should be the same within any given element of the text. For example, all subject heads should look the same, all footnotes should match, etc.

Footnotes: Abbreviate "fn." Footnotes give added meaning or clarification for a word, phrase, or verse. These are copyrighted per translation.

Fouled Firsts/Working Proofs: When a proof is marked for correction, it becomes "fouled." When typesetters make corrections that are noted on fouled firsts, they are likely to create second pages (or *clean* seconds).

Front Matter: Material preceding the main text, such as the copyright page, table of contents, and preface. It may also include additional articles. These pages are usually numbered in lowercase Roman numerals; the half-title page and the title page are counted, but no number is on them; the first page number shown may be *iii*, for example. The table of contents lists only the sections following it, not those preceding it.

Galleys: These are usually typeset pages, just not in the final layout of the pages. They are often used to proof features before they are complete or articles before they are added to the full Bible. Sometimes galleys are created to create a castoff for the page count.

Garner's: *Garner's Modern American Usage.* The 4th edition was published in 2016. It was written by Bryan A. Garner, who wrote the grammar section of the CMS. It is an excellent resource for grammar/punctuation questions.

Globally: If there is a pattern error, it can often be fixed by the typesetter just by making a global adjustment or search and replace.

Gutter: This is the inside margin of the page. It is where the binding will ultimately be. In many cases the margin outside the working area is larger on the gutter side.

Half-Title Page: If present, the half-title page is usually page *i* of any book. Only the title of the book without the subtitle appears there. Many Bibles have introductory pages to the Old and New Testament that are also called half-title pages.

Hang: This term is usually used to refer to quotation marks, sigla, and, sometimes, verse numbers that fall outside the poetry or special setting indent—they "hang."

Hard Hyphen: A hyphen that is required in the word as part of its spelling (orthographic), e.g., Kadesh-Barnea, as opposed to a soft hyphen, which is in a word because it broke at the end of a line.

Hole (or Lake or River): This is a noticeable group of spaces between words on several lines that looks like a hole or lake or river.

Hr# (Hair Space): This is a thin, narrow space that can be added when two characters are touching. This is often used between single and double quotation marks or a quotation mark and punctuation.

Justify: A line or section that goes all the way to the right margin of the page or column. If it is full justified, it runs from the left margin to the right margin and there is equal space between all words per line. Left justified means it aligns at the left margin and the right side is ragged right and there is equal space between all words in the whole section. Right justified means it aligns at the right margin and the left side is ragged. This usually only occurs in flush right lines. Bottom justified means that the text should reach the bottom of the page.

Kerning: This is a narrowing of the space between letters or numbers so that they fit together better and less space is between the characters. It is especially noticeable where the "a" tucks under the "Y" and "V." Typesetters often adjust kerning to make lines tighter or more readable

Leader Dots: These are a row of dots that visually connect the chapter titles and section headings to their corresponding page numbers. These are often found in a table of contents and go from the book or chapter title over to the page number. A concordance should require at least two leader dots per line if they are used.

Leading (pronounced "ledding"): The horizontal space between lines of text that needs to be equal.

Letter Spacing: This is the space between letters (see kerning). The typesetters sometimes vary this to make the page fit all the parameters of the job.

Ligature: This is when two or more letters are joined together on purpose. Example: ff.

Line Spaces: This is the space between the lines of text. See Leading.

Liquid Els: Words that end in "le" when the last syllable only makes an "el" sound. Words such as *dou-ble* or *trou-ble*. Some publishers do not want these as a separate syllable in their word breaks.

Loose Lines: Lines with extra spacing between the words or letters that become distracting to the reader. These can be unavoidable in Bibles with narrow columns. See Tight Lines.

Map: This is a master list of all the supplemental features for a project and where they should be located (by what Scripture passage). Use this to check that all the features are present and in the correct locations.

Missing Text: A term used when a part of a verse or footnote is missing.

M-W/Merriam-Webster's: Currently the 11th edition. Used to determine proper word breaks.

Oblique: This refers to text that is tilted or

slanted. This can be confused as italic text, but they are not the same. See these examples:

- *This is an example of oblique text.*
- *This is an example of italic text.*

The easiest way to spot the difference is the letter *a*. True italic text is easier to read and is usually preferred.

Orphan: The first line of a paragraph stranded at the *bottom* of a page or column. Contrast Widow.

Parallel Passages: Passages that refer to the same or similar text in the Bible. These are often placed under the subject head. Sometimes in cross-references they are listed with the symbol // for parallel lines.

Pica: See Points.

Pilcrow: The paragraph indicator (¶) that often appears in KJV Bibles.

Poetry: The lines begin at different levels, called primary, secondary, and tertiary. If any of these levels is too long for the margin, they turn over (or "spill over") to a fourth level, called the turnover position. These four positions must always be at the same place for any given project.

Points: This is the standard of measurement that we use for all setting indents (there are 72 points in an inch). Do not confuse "points" with "picas" (a pica is 12 points).

Preferred Breaks: Each translation has preferred word breaks. For example, some translations prefer to break *Pha-raoh* while others prefer *Phar-aoh*.

Print Signature: A signature is a group of pages that are printed, most likely on both sides of a single sheet of paper, that, once folded, trimmed, bound, and cut, become a specific number of pages. Bibles are usually printed on 48- or 64-page signatures, which means adjustments may be needed to avoid extra blank pages. Bibles can often be printed with a final half signature or quarter signature to help alleviate page count concerns.

Proof: This is a printout of what will appear in the book.

Prose: This is regular text (usually narrative). It can either have a paragraph indent or be flush left (all the way to the left margin). The right margin can also be either full justified or ragged right.

Psalm Notes/Titles: These are different from subject heads. They are the introductory notes in some psalms that tell the incident that caused the writer to compose the psalm (see Psalm 3).

Query/Question: This is a a question for the editor.

Ragged Right: This is used in some special settings and in some Bibles for prose. The right margin is not justified, and there are usually no word breaks except at hard hyphens.

Read for Sense: The process of reading and checking copy only when something doesn't seem right.

Recto: The right side of the spread or page.

Recto Breaks: A word break where part of the word is on the right/recto page and the rest is on the left/verso page of the next spread. Some publishers like to avoid this.

Red Letter: These are the words of Christ in the NT that often appear in red ink. Some translations will also have the words of Christ in red when they are being quoted by another person. See Mark 14:72, where Peter is remembering Christ's words. Some will not include the words of Christ in red after he ascended (e.g., in Revelation).

Right Justified: The text aligns on the right

margin. Some Bibles have all prose right justified, and some are ragged right.

River: A space between words in several lines that looks like a river going down the page.

Roman Font: This is the normal font for the project with no italics.

Roman Numerals: Letters representing numbers. I is 1, V is 5, X is 10, etc. As opposed to Arabic numerals.

Rule: In typesetting a straight line is called a rule. A "cut-off rule" is a short rule sometimes found at the bottom of a page above footnotes.

Run Back: Move something back to the previous line.

Run On: Put the text from two lines together, being sure to add the appropriate spaces.

Run-On Chapter: This is where a paragraph continues from one chapter to another and the text runs on to the verse 1 of the next chapter and there is no line break. Even though other chapters may not have a verse number 1, a run-on chapter will. See Exodus 8:1 or John 8:1 in the NIV for examples.

Run Over: This means to move a word to the following line.

Running Foot: When the info that would be in a running head is at the bottom of the page.

Running Head: The information at the top of the page that shows the book, chapter, and sometimes verse beginning on the verso page or ending on the recto page. The verse number usually needs to be on the page to be reflected in the running head. Some projects will have only chapter numbers. Some projects will list a verse number if any text from the verse is on the page; others require the verse number to actually be on the page. The chapter start counts as verse number 1 even if there is no actual verse number there.

SBL/*Society of Biblical Literature Handbook of Style*: This is in the 2nd edition. This is used by many Christian scholars and is the main reference for some projects.

Serial Comma: Also called "Oxford comma." This is the final comma before the "and" or "or" in a series of items (e.g., red, white, and blue).

Sigla (pl.)/ Siglum (sg.): This is the letter or number both in the Scripture and in the footnote/cross-reference section that marks the location of that feature.

Signature: See Print Signature.

Slugging: Comparing proof to the copy by overlapping pages (or folding the proof) and seeing if the last word on each line is the same. This is often done in seconds to make sure no lines have changed on a page from firsts.

Spec (Specification): The measurements for all indents (¶ starts, poetry, special settings), font sizes, etc., for a job.

Special Setting: These can be lists, proclamations, inscriptions, letters, or other unique settings that are not prose or poetry.

Spread: The two-page open book; the verso and recto pages side by side.

Stack: When you run your eye down the margin (left or right) and you see the same word repeated three or four times.

Std # (Standard Space): This is used to indicate that there isn't the same amount of space between chapter numbers and the text, between footnotes, etc.

Stet: This stands for "let it stand" (used as an instruction on a proof to indicate that a correction or alteration should be ignored). It is a comment we use when we don't want the typesetter or publisher to make the change we marked.

Style Manuals: Many translations have style manuals/guides that give some basic rules for how to set the specific translation.

Subject Heads: These are the headings that translators have added to help identify sections of the Bible. They are not Scripture but are copyrighted and must always be included unless permission has been secured to exclude them.

Superscript: Sometimes called "superior." These are raised letters or numbers, usually used as sigla for footnotes or cross-references.

Supplemental (a.k.a. "ancillary"): Anything that is not part of the Scripture text, subject heads, footnotes, or cross-references. This can refer to articles, study notes, or devotional boxes.

Text Notes: Or textual notes. This is another name for footnotes.

Tight Lines: Tight lines are only those with almost no word spaces—almost illegible. See Loose Lines.

Title Page: Often page *iii* in many Bibles and usually includes the complete title and subtitle of the book, the name of the author, editor(s), etc., the edition number, the name of the publisher, the publisher's logo.

Trim Lines: The short horizontal and vertical lines sometimes seen at the corners of proof pages. These show where the page will be trimmed (or cut) to. Sometimes at the top and bottom of the page in the middle there is a circle with what looks like a cross in it. This shows the center of the page.

Unjustify: When a line or section has been set justified when it should be ragged, we mark it to "unjustify."

Verso: The left side of the spread or page.

Widow: Something left alone at the end.

- *A paragraph widow* in prose is a very short word or end of a word that is so short that it doesn't meet up with the paragraph indent following it (the white space). A column widow is when the top of a column begins with the "end" of something—either the short end line of a paragraph, or a turnover line of poetry, or one last line of a list.

- *A page widow* is when there is not enough content on a page. There need to be at least five lines of text in a single-column Bible and three lines each in a double column Bible.

- *A footnote widow* is when there are four or fewer letters alone on a line (this can vary by translation). Also a single number is not allowed on a line by itself. If all footnotes are in one column of a two-column Bible, a widow is less than two characters.

Word Breaks: Most translations have their own word break list based on how the translators have determined what the pronunciations (or syllable breaks) should be and what words are included in their translation.

Word Spaces: Between each word or number (not each digit) there should be one word space. If there is too much space between two words, mark it to be "eq #." If two words are run together, mark it for a "#." *Word space* and *hair space* are not interchangeable.

Protestant Book Numbers
for Bible Books

01 Genesis	34 Nahum
02 Exodus	35 Habakkuk
03 Leviticus	36 Zephaniah
04 Numbers	37 Haggai
05 Deuteronomy	38 Zechariah
06 Joshua	39 Malachi
07 Judges	40 Matthew
08 Ruth	41 Mark
09 1 Samuel	42 Luke
10 2 Samuel	43 John
11 1 Kings	44 Acts
12 2 Kings	45 Romans
13 1 Chronicles	46 1 Corinthians
14 2 Chronicles	47 2 Corinthians
15 Ezra	48 Galatians
16 Nehemiah	49 Ephesians
17 Esther	50 Philippians
18 Job	51 Colossians
19 Psalms	52 1 Thessalonians
20 Proverbs	53 2 Thessalonians
21 Ecclesiastes	54 1 Timothy
22 Song of Solomon	55 2 Timothy
23 Isaiah	56 Titus
24 Jeremiah	57 Philemon
25 Lamentations	58 Hebrews
26 Ezekiel	59 James
27 Daniel	60 1 Peter
28 Hosea	61 2 Peter
29 Joel	62 1 John
30 Amos	63 2 John
31 Obadiah	64 3 John
32 Jonah	65 Jude
33 Micah	66 Revelation

ABOUT PEACHTREE
PUBLISHING SERVICES

OUR MISSION (WHY WE EXIST)
We exist to protect and advance God's Word.

OUR VISION (WHO WE ARE)
Peachtree is a Bible proofreading and editorial company that serves worldwide publishers who desire to create perfect editions of God's Word and other Bible-related books.

CONTACT INFORMATION
Peachtree@PeachtreeEditorial.com
Espanol@PeachtreeEditorial.com
US: +1-770-631-9073

Made in United States
Orlando, FL
23 November 2021

10682007R00068